Sucker4love Too:

"Love Ain't Logical its lyrical"

by

Coolgmack

Sucker4love Too: *"Love Ain't Logical its lyrical"* i

Disclaimer

This book is a blend of fiction and non-fiction. Some names, characters, places, and events are either the product of the author's imagination or are used in a fictionalized manner. Any resemblance to actual persons, living or dead, or actual events is purely coincidental unless explicitly stated otherwise.

The non-fiction portions reflect the author's personal experiences, opinions, and research. They are provided for informational purposes only and are not intended as professional advice, whether medical, legal, financial, or otherwise. The author and publisher make no representations or warranties regarding the accuracy, applicability, or completeness of the content and disclaim any liability arising directly or indirectly from its use.

Readers are encouraged to exercise their own judgment and seek professional advice where appropriate.

ISBN:979-8-9930046-2-4

Cover Design bycoolgmack

Printed in the United States of America

First Edition

Dedication & Acknowledgments

To everyone who's been riding with me since day one — the fans, the friends, and the ones who never stopped believing in me — this one's for you.

To all the women in my family, thank you for loving me so deeply that "love" became a healthy addiction. Your strength and warmth shaped who I am. A special shoutout to my aunty/mom Shirley and my grandma — your love, your advice, and yes, even telling me not to cuss — always kept me grounded. You are the foundation I stand on.

To my undercover haters — thank you too. Your doubt is my motivation. Your fuel is what drives me harder.

To God — thank you for protecting me through jail and through hell on earth. You never left my side, and you blessed me with effortless talents I'll never take for granted.

To Kobe — your "Black Mamba Mentality" lives in me. I don't care if I'm down 20, I'm still shooting for 81. You taught me to never quit, no matter the score. Rest easy, legend.

To the women who broke my heart, and to the ones whose hearts I broke — thank you. Love and pain both taught me how to grow. Good thing a heart can heal.

This book is my way of saying: I see you. I feel you. And I'm still here — writing, loving, living.

Like Father Like Son

In memory of you, Dad, I carry on your legacy. Your spirit lives in me—spiritually, lyrically, and genetically. You taught me how to hustle, to be wise with my money, lessons I'll never forget, as priceless as loving me.

When it rains, I feel your presence, a sprinkle on my soul, and I find myself clutching this gold, sipping on this rose, reminiscing on the stroll, walking with a confident goal, posing to get chose—I'm supposed to get chose.

Never faking it, just living life as I'm supposed,
never taking it. I go and make my own doe
I'm a man made in God's image, no flaws, no pretense, no gimmicks, just a plan, a habit, and a blessing from heaven's kiss.

You taught me to be strong, to move on from those who don't get it. "No" is just short for "not right now," so Imma always go and get it. I'm not the type to beg, I stand out, I'm terrific. I will hustle in the trenches even when I'm inflicted.

When I asked for help,
my frenemies turned their back,
but I never knelt—
I lived it. That's facts.

You taught me to play every hand I was dealt with grace, to face the trenches with a poker face, never feeling disgraced for asking for help, knowing they would hate. You said they'd act strange when I changed, and that they'd stay the same.

You told me, "God don't like ugly,"
and since I'm handsome, He must love me.

You taught me to face my problems,
to solve them, to never run,
and that if I pray, my worries would fade,
for I am your son.

When I got locked up on false charges,
I had to fight back.
Those charges I had to beat it,
but they wouldn't leave me alone, like I'm Mikejax,

They are knowing I’m Mr. Thrilla.
I ain’t no killer, but I'm always determined to get even,
because success is the best revenge, and I believe in it.

I'm impatient for karma, so my anxiety can get the best of me, but thanks, Dad, for communicating with my spirit,
even though you never met me.

I know it wasn't your fault;
I learned from our spiritual talks how to walk,
you're in my heart by default, holding down the fort.

I'll carry the torch,
build on the foundation we fought,
I learn from the battles, they were for a cause.
those were the lessons you taught, forevermore.

So, when the nights get heavy and the silence gets loud, I hear your voice in my chest like thunder behind the clouds.

I walk with your wisdom sewn in my soul
and stitched into my stride.
Your hustle's in my veins; your pride's in my eyes.

They say grief fades, but I wear it like armor
not to mourn ya, but to honor.
I thank you for making me father.

4

You never held me, but you built me.
You never met me, but you filled me.

And now I stand—flawed, fierce, and chosen
a living echo of the man who taught me
how to turn pain into motion.

Rest in power, Dad.
Your ghost doesn’t haunt me—it guides me.
And I’ll keep rising 'til the whole world recognizes
who lit the fire inside me.

Ray Charles

Like a ray from the sun,
you beam through the clouds,
a fresh breath of air,
you stand out from the crowds.
You're my peace and my power,
your words give me strength.
I refuse to cease; I increase by the hour.
When I'm around you,
I feel more comfortable and complete.
Before I met you,
I seemed to have lost all control of my soul,
I was weak.

My heart was slowly leaking,
I was so defeated.
My motives were depleted.
My life had no meaning.
But when I looked into your eyes,
I saw the sun rise.
I felt like the middle of July in the summertime.
That's the best way for me to describe you.
You were better than any medicine
That a doctor could prescribe you.
You heal every sickness with your presence.
You're the answer to life's lessons.
You're spiritually right,
You have no vice; you're a blessing.
When I was stressing,
my problems, you made me forget them.
You lifted me up on a podium,

helped me rise out of the place I was left in.
for a whole week, in a state of depression.
The Seroquils didn't work;
they just made me keep sweating
in the bed that I slept in.
But you stepped in.
You took charge with a prayer regimen,
You showed me that no meds were better than...

7

"Our Father... which art in heaven."
Christ is like a bread that is forever leavened.

At first, I was half-stepping,
but after we started sexing,
it was great and energetic.
I got the message.

You exceeded my expectations.
I was blessed with great elation.
Your success tastes amazing.
And in your arms,
I have finally found my home,
a love so true, I'll never have to roam.
You are the warmth that fills an empty space,
the perfect melody that time cannot erase.

You are the calm that came after the storm,
the anchor that holds me down
steady and strong.
With you, I am whole,
and my soul sings a song
of pure and endless love goals.
We will see where this love goes.

9

Shoulda Been a Better Son

I shoulda been a better son—
I'm sorry, Mommy, but I failed.
Instead of Grambling State & Yale,
I graduated from the streets,
gambling with base, then went straight to jail.

I was addicted to the fast life,
hustling & women—
that life only led me
to drugging and prison.
I'm sorry, Mommy,
I shoulda been a better son,
but I was playing with them guns,
preying with the thugs.
I shoulda called you more,
but attention—I paid you none.
I was embarrassed
because of your addiction—
I used to run.
But I shoulda showed more love
instead of being the missing son.
I was in the streets hard,
you never knew my whereabouts.
I'm sorry, Mommy,

for having you worry about me
when I was never in the house.

I shoulda been a better son.
Instead of buying you cigs and loosies,
pacifying your addiction to nicotine,
I shoulda hidden them,
or taken away those stogies
that you didn't need.
When I used to see you cough up a lung,
I shoulda flung that vape.
I shoulda been more tough,
not let you touch that base.
I'm sorry, Mommy—
I shoulda been a better son.
Instead of telling you my dreams from my mouth,
I shoulda put them in action,
brought you a dream house.
I shoulda made it in entertainment,
not been a jailbird.
I shoulda kept my word—
but I kept getting high myself
whenever I felt the urge.
Now I'm in a jail cell for a VOP,
and you're in the hospital.

11

I can't even visit when you're weak.
I coulda been the strength that you need.
I wish I coulda kissed your cheeks—
Mommy, you are so sweet.

I'm sorry, Mommy,
I coulda been a better son.
But I had you worrying about me,
watching me high and stuttering.
You were scared I'd get shot up,
locked up, or jumped again.
I was going bonkers in Yonkers.
You told me to stay in the house,
but I was always out—
smoking & joking,
then showing up in the morning at your house,
trying to sleep on your couch.
I'm sorry, Mommy,
I shoulda been a better son.
I shoulda been realer—
shoulda shot or killed off
all your drug dealers.
I shoulda forced you into inpatient
so you could heal up…

’cause when you’re sober,
you show more love to me.
I shoulda been sterner
in instilling your recovery.

I’m sorry, Mommy,
I shoulda been a better son.
I shoulda been leading by example to prove.
But seeing me high
only gave you an excuse to use too.
I was a damn fool.
It was hard for me to stop
when I couldn’t apply it to myself.
I relied on substances,
lied about hustling—
I needed some help.

I’m sorry, Mommy,
I coulda been a better son.
I failed…
Now I’m in Valhalla,
in the county jail,
sending this letter through the mail.
I’m sorry, Mommy.
But I hope that you are doing well.

Let Me Know

Don't be subtle with me
if you wanna cuddle with me,
It's hard to read body signs
when I'm chasing dollar signs—what it's gonna be?

Just let me know if your body's meant to be mine,
They say if it's wholeheartedly,
then affection robbery ain't a crime.

If not, I'll let you go—
But we could grow into a tree,

started with a seed I planted in your soil,
though polluted with weeds.
I'll always be loyal,
But you gotta let me know,
So, we can rise to the highest heights—
Love can change your life, for sure.
But you are playing that hard-to-get type…
I just wanna take you from good to great,
But you hesitate to sacrifice.

Let me know—I'll be patient,
Like a resident in John Hopkins, like Anthony,
Silently, like a lamb, waiting for you to answer me.

My heart's been vacant like a lot in Harlem,
I like you a lot, you are beautiful and charming,
But you treat me like I'm a piece of Charmin.
When I'm in your grill like Foreman,
Around your friends you be performing,
Acting like you don't notice me… ignoring.
Claiming you ain't looking for a man,
But all you do is work, and sham
and your weekends be bland—boring!!!

Let me know, I can't read your mind,

But do know I'm the type of guy that you like.
I catch the subtle signs when it's just us two, alone—
You get nervous, start pulling out your phone.
Searching for distraction,
Fighting the satisfaction,

of attraction to this passion of blackness.
They say once you go black,
you ain't ever going backwards,
That's a fact, miss—
Have you doing backflips on your mattress.

So let me know—no hesitation, no disguise,
I see that fire and desire in your eyes.
Even though you tired, you really can't hide.
We could rise above the weeds,
Bloom to the skies,
from a seed to a tree—watch our empire multiply.
I'll ride with you through the storms, calm and wise,
With a sober mind that's steady,
And a love that never dies.

It's your move, your call—the rest is fate.
Step up, take my hand, let's elevate…
And let the haters hate.

Set It Up For Me

I miss her.
I wish her type of man
was more like me,
so I could kiss her.
I could be anything in this world
I wanted to be—
except for hers.
Make this make sense to her.
You, her best friend—
can you talk to her for me?
Tell her how good I will be.
Like sugar to her IV—
so steady.
so sweet,

I will put everything beneath her.
A beautiful queen is what I see.
I need her.
I will feed her—physically, mentally.
I feel this is meant to be.
Please, set it up for her and me
to be in the same vicinity.
I want the chance

to give her the same enthusiasm
she gives to me.
I guarantee,
she would not want to get rid of me.

I'm not saying I am the best,
but I can treat her better than her ex
who used to beat her,
keep her in distress,
in duress.
I will accept all her baggage—
her flaws, her scars,
everything else involved.
I will love her with a passion
and help her through her withdrawals.
I know, sometimes people
get addicted to relationships,
thinking pain is love,
getting lost in the mix.
I get it.
I'm not a judge, not a critic.
I will do more than budge when times get tough.
I will stand side by side with her.
I would have come to her myself,
but I am shy. besides
I didn't know if she was seeing another guy.

19

I have a fear of rejection—
I care about perception,
I didn't want to make things weird
with the receptionist.
Right now,
when we talk, it's only cordial.
I don't want to make the wrong move.
That's why I called on you.

Do me this one favor—I'll pay you—
put in a good word for me.
I've changed all my player behaviors.
I'm looking to settle down,
trade vows.
I want a whole family,
a queen to wear my crown.

See if she has a number for me,
or her IG.
Ask her how she feels about me
or if she even like me?

If so, Friday see if she's free
for dinner and a movie—my treat?
Let me know.
I'll be waiting, in anticipation.
Please be discreet.

The less people know, the better.
I didn't want to sweat her,
but give her this poem/love letter.

Let her know I will be waiting for her response.
Even if it's a dub, I'll remain cool,
collected and calm,

I couldn't pass up this opportunity
for her and me to be in unity.
Risking my position—
worth every bit of it.

Truthfully,
she is so beautiful to me,
with all the qualities of a wife.
What she does to me—
I never felt before in my life.

Thanks, sis.
I appreciate you for making these moves.
Soon, we'll be lit, in Jamaica, on a cruise.

Work your matchmaking magic for me.
I like her—very much.
Like MJB:
she is all that I need.

21

A Different World

I wanna walk with you, can I talk to you?
I just wanna know your aim
I don't wanna play games.
My last name, I wanna offer you...
I'm not the type to force you;
of course, you
have the choice
to love me or dub me,
it's yours to choose.
Luckily,
I’ve been dodging chicks chasing me,
to be with you, my boo, yeah you
that’s factually true.
Even though we just met
I fell in love with you,
can’t be subtle with you.
I wanna cuddle with you,
and on rainy nights
watch the puddles with you.
I’ll be heroic or chauvinistic,
whatever you want to do
I'm sorry—when I touch you,
does it make you uncomfortable?
I'm just trying to comfort you,

get to know you better.
I'll say whatever, I have to say
to reach that treasure,

Then act like I never met ya
then I'll probably forget your name,
After I get what I want,
with the same ole game
you see that lump in my pants?
I'll shift the circumstance
just to work my hands...
on your body—
I want you to be my mommy.
I'll like all your hobbies,
we can make out in the lobby.
I'm usually, or probably,
slipped myself a Molly
just to get it crackin' like Polly.

Hennessy mixed with laughter
got us doing whatever after.
We're both horn dog catchers
hoping the passion moves us faster.

You're half Black, half Spanish, and fly—
but this curve will send you
to a different world

like Jasmine's guy.
If loving you is a crime,
I'm guilty of my innocence.
This Hennessy got us delirious,
and that cat got you curious.

Can't focus on our memories
remember we—mmm, forget it.
My name is Eric Derrick,
this night we'll cherish.

With due diligence,
I'll let Mr. Thriller
play with your intelligence,
put you under my spell witch
I can smell a freaky chick quick.
You couldn't tell that I'm not rich
by my knock-off pendants.
I'll sit and sip,
let the Hennessy kick in.
I never act timid like Tim—
let's spur this moment.
If you're good,
I'll let you feel on my big bonus
like you own it.

24

I got enough cojones to say things,
thanks to the courage from this drink.
Let’s go for a sneaky link
while we’re tipsy, no time to think.
And before you know it,
you’re bent over my mama’s sink,
screaming for God,
signing my back
with my blood as your ink.

But as the night bled into morning,
I didn’t just want your body
I wanted your story,
your warming, your scars.
I wanted to hold you
when the liquor wore off.

I want to kiss you
when the silence returned,
and promise that even
if this started reckless,
it could end in something that would burn...

Hope-less Romance

When I look into your eyes,
you make my heart cry,
because I…
been looking for you all my life.
I spent dark nights praying for a wife,
then you came as a light
at the end of the longest tunnel,
shining like a beacon—
I wonder if we can cuddle.

You're like freedom to a lifer,
Peter to a piper.
Only if we can decipher

the weeds in wild hun,
because when you smile, hun

I see miles of happiness with no rebuttal.
I wanna know you inside out and love you,
I wanna be the missing piece to your puzzle.
You make me never wanna get into trouble.
I want to assist you
to do all the things you want to do.

You've got this charm and aura
that makes me wanna see more of ya.
I'd swim to Florida
to find the keys to your heart, if you called up

I know you probably have issues with trust,
and you don't trust dudes.
Sweetheart I get you.
I don't trust dudes too

But when I'm with you, the time stops
you make the hands vanish off the clock.
Don't care about the haters, let them watch
It feels like it's just us two ✌ you and me
a V like 10:10.
a victory,

I grin as I watch you take my order,
I'll support you to the end.

27

My head spins like waves in your water
I wanna be more than your friend.

I wanna know everything you're about,
I never want to see you lonely
I never want to see you do without
You're like water in a drought,
CPR to a mouth-to-mouth,

a fresh breath of air…
I can tell you're not from here,
probably from somewhere down south.
You gave me hope when I was in despair.
I feel chills when you're near.

Ouch… gotta pinch myself, I must be dreaming
to get this close to a goddess gleaming
as I approach. This serene Venus

Your smile shines like a chandelier…
I know you don't care,
because every man is in your ear
telling you what you want to hear.
you may think that I'm weird,
becase I wanna give you more than a cheer.
We can wait for a year
and pray over our fears

Hopefully,
when those checks get cleared,
I can take you up out of here
In a leer— one wish
I'll give you a fishing pole
so you can get your own fish
But I understand
that you may not be free at the moment…
So I'll be patient,
I've got enough skills to cope.with
If I'm the one you want to grow with,
I'd never let you have an opponent,
or mess up your focus.
Hopefully, I'm chosen
to be your man,
or whatever you want me to be
it's in your hands.
Even if it's as an associate,
all I know is this:
I'm a great man with a great plan,
that would feed you grapes from my land.
just give me the notion.
Until I get that answer,
I'll leave that door open…
while I'm hoping.
Impatient like a cancer ●

Golden Seal

I remember when we met, I was thirsty,
tried to have sex on the first day.
You rejected it, but I had to respect it,
even though I was vexed, I had to accept it.

You were like sunlight's ray, a brand-new day,
reversed my cravings, helped me find my way.
I was amazed someone took the time to say… hey,
and from that point, you helped my mind elevate.

Clouds were no longer gray,
sun rays shining on your face.
I saw light at the end of the tunnel—
I got out that grave.
Thanks for showing me
the beautiful road that God has paved.
With hope, I prayed…
my future wasn't strange.
I turned from my negative ways,
I never went astray,
in fact still working on change
to this very day.

I put that negative energy into positivity
I can see it, it's possible to achieve.
The mission wasn't impossible,
I just had to stop my woes,
funnel that energy into me.

Even in prison, they couldn't lock up my soul.
You showed me how to care for me.
Even with lots of parole
I didn't let oppression make me fear to achieve.
I knew I could succeed
without others controlling what I eat.
I hold my destiny… yes, I'm free.

All I had to do was trust God and invest in me.
You showed me the ingredients, the recipe.
The rest is history.

Judicial weapons weren't prosperous against me.
I didn't let HIS-story
dictate how I'd live and breathe.

When I finally was physically free,
being with my family meant the world to me.
Most friends left me to rot in pee—
went on with their life and forgot about me.

But you helped me unlock my heart without a key.

Even when my own ocks doubted me,
you never let me go hungry, let me eat.
Not just financially…
you understood my needs.

You gave me seeds that could grow into a tree,
our roots were planted deep,
you helped me out of that hell creek,
and gave me wisdom as water, that's peace

you told me that I could fish with my own pole,
and stand tall on my own two feet.

You didn't give me fish,
but helped me fish through currentcy.

You helped me escape like Jonah
through the beast's teeth.

Your companionship never ran
from the ships at sea.

You helped me start my own company,
gave me deep love by keeping me company.
Comforted me when the opps tried to come for me,
helped me sort priorities,

my wants from my needs.

Even when my mind was hazed from blunts,
you stayed through your dismays, never gave up

You gave me everything I wanted.
That was real.
I'll always appreciate you,
and be loyal—I must, that's how I feel.

That's just how I'mma give it up.
I'mma have love for you no matter what.
One thing for sure:
our bond will never rust.

Regrets I Confess

I feel lost without you.
The thought of life without you
sounds crazy.
I must admit, I miss you and feel so remorseful.

You know I adore you.
I felt like I was forced
into a corner, and I got tossed into

A mind state.
I said things that I didn't mean.
That was my mistake.
It was awful, not thoughtful, and mean.

I was sleeping my life away in a daze.
My words weren't thought through.
I was coming down a mountain of haze,
trying to kick that habit to the curb.
I should've sought you.

It was the nerves of me
to not give you what you need.
Now I caught the flu.
I'm sick, with symptoms of COVID.
Hopefully I can get over this.
I wish I could just hold and kiss
those sweet lips
and once again taste your sweetness.

I hope that you're not mad at me.
I was trying to just be me,
not expressing what I wanted to say exactly.
I was half asleep…

I didn't mean to say those words.
That was bad; I didn't mean to be a creep.
I had a dream…
rather, it was a nightmare seen.

When I awoke, you weren't right there with me
between my sheets.
I'm weak…

35

I'm sorry.
I'm asking for another chance, as I speak.
My love for you is deep.
I just needed space to see.
I hated to see you leave.

I'll pay for your flight right back to me
so we can make up and make love like how it’s
supposed to be.
I want to feel you close to me.
I didn’t want to hurt you again—this is my apology.

I'll follow your lead.
I want to be the only man that you need.
I promise not to look to other fishes in the sea.

I stand on that decision, baby.
I'm done with other ladies; they can never be
what you are to me.
Wholeheartedly,
I’m so sorry.
Please accept my apologies

Someone

In my life I need that someone

Someone who will wipe away my tears

Someone who will listen to my fears

Someone who will be full of care

Someone who will always be there
Someone who will understand

Someone who will be my helping hand

Someone who I can trust with my heart

Someone who won't rip it apart

Someone who will love me for who I am

Someone who will be a part of God's plan

Someone who I can laugh and cry with

Someone who will always be my sidekick

Someone who's love for me will never die

Someone who won't cheat on me or lie

Someone who will always be true

I really hope that someone is you

Cryonics 2

She broke me in places that no one could see, with whispers like blades that cut deep but quietly. Her silence was louder than thunder's roar, yet still, I kept knocking on her broken, closed door. She loved me — I know — in her own way, but love can bruise when it doesn't stay. She held my heart like fragile glass, then let it slip and watched the pieces pass.

I saw the ache behind her eyes, the kind that hides beneath the "hi's" and the "goodbyes." She wanted peace of mind, but our love war was toxic. Now my heart's in deeper cryonics, frozen in time, caught in a relationship that's ironic. You were my pulse, my breath, but your warmth turned cold, like death.

All my friends just watched me as my heart unfolded when she left. She was my rhythm, my heartbeat's miss, stepping on my dreams and stealing my bliss. Her needs replaced the life I needed; my spirit drained, my hope depleted. No breath, no pause, no chance to rest. Every moment was a test, a war in my chest. Arguments sparked, then another chance lost, like dancing in the fire without counting the cost. I gave her mornings and midnight prayers, but she gave me mourning and vacant stares.

Yet still, I stayed with her through the aches and the stings, because love isn't always gentle. And yet — I swear you loved me too. I was caught in a burning, a fleeting truth. We were shattered but strangely whole, two jagged halves, one battered soul. I stayed not from weakness but because love doesn't just let go; even when bleeding, I couldn't say no. When a rose sows its seeds, even through weeds, it still believes.

She cried in circles that I couldn't reach. Her pain had a language she would never teach, but I learned it anyway line by line, every sigh, every pause, every sign. I did everything right, just to make her mine. I loved her through the storm's embrace, through nights too cold for me to face. And I knew that she loved me too — I felt it burn, even when she swore, she would leave and never return.

We are a story carved in scars, in midnight prayers and falling stars. We played through all the cards, fought the odds. It was not clean, it was not kind, not neatly designed, but love like ours is hard to find. So, if she walks or if she stays, I'll love her anyway through the darkest maze. Some hearts, though torn apart, still beat together. But mine just stopped. I'm weak forever.

New Addiction

(CoolGmack)
If this isn't love, then why do I feel this way?
Every day it's a new addiction I crave
She talks... I listen to what she says
Her walk is vicious.... attention I pay

(Slowmtion)
So here I lay
Dreams unfulfilled
Plans we build
There is no question why I feel this way
And my heart's love will never go astray
She's just that new edition

Add her to my heart I'm wishing
I made plans, and she understands
Why must it be this way
And all her attention I pay

(CoolGmack)
With her permission I stayed
She's my sunshine after tremendous rain
I rather live in a cave than to betray
her loyalty is never estranged
To God I give the thanks
she's the answer to all the days I preyed and prayed

(Slowmtion)
Why do I feel this way?
We fit like a glove,
now we both know love
The strongest kind
Us two combined
The world notices us
True love, is definitely necessary to discuss

(CoolGmack)
It was February, when we first hooked up
You have that good good love
I remembered.......
you was so tight it fitted like a glove

Loving you was right it was bliss we touched
We never wanted to sever
that's when I knew that night
you were sent from the heavens above

(Slowmtion)
She is that piece of mind her piece is mine
Her and I ideas combined
Now the question is if it isn't love
then why do we feel this way

There is we, that understand... the crazy
Tame but torn
We are reborn
Love the rebirth
Having no doubts
on why we were put here on this Earth

Love is Everything
So together this song we Sang
Our relationship
Our hop to our hip
We are the new edition
Stop..... look and listen

Together We Rise

I was just going outside
to bring the food in.
Why do I have to come back
to attitude and rudeness again?

I wasn't outside chasing chicks;
I was chasing checks
to put food on the table
Trying to erase our debt

I don't get it;

why do you gotta adhere to the critics?
Then you want me to give my full attention
to hear all the bullspit...
Tell them foes to mind their business
Or find a mistress
tell them to not hate
if they're not happy in their own relationships

Isn't it my bread and glasses
that's going on the napkins?
I don't understand this madness,
but imma let you have it.
The last word
for the sake of no arguments,
I'm going to park the whip,
Before our car flips

Imma pump my brakes and take a loss
so, the kids don't see us in distraught
Luckily, they never saw when we fought.
It's always my fault,
and somehow, I gotta pay the cost
to make it peaceful in the house.
I guess my wallet is the boss.
I remember when you tried divorce
when I was forced

in the wilderness of the system.
Maybe it was your dementia
or forgetfulness.
You have selective memory
when you like to mention shit.

It will be better in the future
when you realize
That I am the protector,
the provider, and the super.

But you do good, huh?
You like to bring up my past
of course you did.
I stayed because
I don't want my seeds
to have to grow up in an orphanage.

It's always the same subject;
I'm off this, I'm tired of talking.
If you want to leave me,
go pack your bags and start walking.
You stay bluffing for nothing;
stop fronting.
Can we be a happy family

without being in dysfunction?
I'm just your husband
the one you chose
to take an oath in front of the public.
The one who made you into something
when you were nothing.

So can we just let go
and let God so we can heal?
Keep our circle tight and chill.

I will make love to you
like a husband do.
Cuddle and comfort you,
just make sure our household is comfortable.

No more bickering and arguments...
let's concentrate on being great,
and move into a house
and out of this apartment.

Together we rise, together we stand
Family first, I'll always hold your hand.

Priceless Love

She's more than an ad,
but she will add to your life
that's how it's supposed to be.

She's not commercial, nor is she free,
but she will work for you… for a fee.
Socially, you should—and could
appreciate her vocally.
Approach her with grace,
approach her with speed.

She will help you get out of your mess,
your predicament,
and the proceeds will be priceless…
if you take her advice, miss.

Use the money you could have spent
on your right wrist
and invest it in change, in growth,
in becoming a better chick.

That price doesn't fit.
Those bracelets? Not so sacred.
You've been paying for a show,
a fleeting display of self-hatred.
a story told for the crowd.
She offers a different truth
one that's quiet, and not so loud.

Her value isn't something you can wear
or tag in a post.

She's the life you've always wanted to live,
not the one you brag and boast.
she's always standing on her biz

So, choose to be wise, not just wealthy.
Stop chasing what glitters

and start building what's healthy.
Her worth is found not in numbers,
but in the peace you can find.
she will pull you up when you are under
And that's a profit far greater
than anything of its kind.

Hold her close, cherish her soul,
love her as she loves you,
she will share her role
fully, completely, endlessly.
For she is the life you were meant breathe,

And together, you will rise,
hand in hand, heart to heart, eye to eye
building a love that lasts forever.
That will never sever for life.

My Only True Crime

My love, I see you in my thoughts and dreams. When I wake, I realize just how real you are to me, even if you're not here to comfort me yet. Soon, I hope you will be. No one else truly knows me the way you do or understands me the way you can. You have my whole heart, my mind, and my trust in your hands.

You own my love completely. I'm coming home soon, and when I do, I want your house to become our home. Inside these walls I'm doing my time, but no matter what I go through, you never leave my mind. Not being there with you is my only true crime, but Miss Amerikkka always finds another excuse to keep me behind.

Others in my life may come and go, but you — you are my constant. I know your love is true. I may not be rich, or the most handsome man, but my love for you is deeper than any of that. You are my hun, my heart, my everything.

You light up my life every time you answer my call, and when the time runs out, I fall. You are my stars and my moon, and I hold on to the promise that being with you will come very soon.

So, when you lay your head down at night, take this to heart: no one, and nothing, will ever keep us apart

Baby, It's Gonna Be Alright

Baby, touch my face with your gentle hue. When I have a day, I feel I can't get through, I think of you. All I have to do is close my eyes, and feel you close to me touching me softly, sweetly, pulling me into your arms, where I'm supposed to be. I love to hear you whispering, *"Baby, it's gonna be alright."*

You stroke my waves and touch my face with your gentle touch. Then you slide your hands down my pants and say, *"Baby, I want you so much."*

I can feel the warmth of your body as we hold each other close. You look into my eyes and tell me, *"Baby, I want you the most."*

You whisper in my ear, my heart fills with belief and hope. You encourage me to stay strong, to have faith, to cope. Your love is helping me find the strength I need to fight. When I feel it's too much, when I can't go on,
I hear you say, *"Baby, it's gonna be alright."*
I love you, sweetheart, and I want and need you in my life. No one can replace you, and hopefully, one day, you'll be my wife. **Baby, It's Gonna Be Alright**

New Leaves

Miss, I hope my persistence doesn't become a burden, you are perfect, I think you are worth it. They say respect is given, but love, you have to earn it. So, I'm trying my earnest, vying for you because I feel you deserve it.

I'm determined to show you why you need me in your life, so I can satisfy your body, soul, and your mind. Why don't you give us a try?

Yet you seem to be taken aback, waiting for someone else who isn't coming back-- or sleeping on me, taking a nap.

Why reach for the moon, when you have a star in your hands? Why trek to a foreign land when I'm right here where you stand? This could be a part of God's plan.

It can't be a coincidence that we're existing in the same place at the same time, yearning for love. I can make this make sense. I can tell that you're skeptical and suspicious, because of other men being inconsistent, but I want you to know that was them—I am him!!!

You tried the rest, now ride with the best. I'm not trying to apply the press, but I am striving for a yes. When are you going to realize what's in front of your face, instead of looking back to the past, which is full of lies, waste, and mistakes?

Miss, I hate to break the news, but that's the space that they're taking. It will have you dazed and confused That's why I had to make a move, to pursue you.

You're too beautiful to be living life by yourself. That's like a book unread that's stuck on the shelf. We all need some help.

I can understand when you say you don't want a man because of all the pain that you've felt. At least accept a helping hand, because you can't make a change all by yourself.

Please don't be angry at me because of what others did before me. I would never cross you, I will hold it like a rosary, so I don't know why you've chosen to oppose me. The old me is history. Don't let my past acts precede me. Give yourself a chance for romance, because even a tree can grow new leaves.

MY FEELINGS FOR YOU

How I yearn for your warm embrace
Tears fall down my face
The look in my eyes
Cannot hide the love I have inside
I think about you all the time
I know in the end we will be just fine

Touch me...Love me…be with me
The way we are supposed to be
I forever want to be with you
And do the things that lovers do

Tell me you want to be with me
And that we are meant to be
Ferocious pain goes away
Please don't come back another day
You take away all my worries
With you, nothing can hurt me

Dreaming of you
Is all I do
This fire I feel... sparks...heat...passion…burning.
My feelings for you I cannot hide
Wishing. Hoping...yearning...

Wanting — needing you near
I long for the day when you are here
It's my vision, my dream
and its oh so clear
It's you… whom I adore
It's you whom I long for
I just want to give you my love
my heart
And I never want us to be apart

Every night I lay in bed
wishing you were there
But your somewhere else
Instead of being here

One day I will feel your warm embrace
And no more tears will fall down my face
Baby, I love and miss you
with all my heart and soul <3<3<3<3

Mami Te amo y extrano con todo mi corazon y mi aima
Mi corazón estaba roto, tú me hiciste completo.

That Special Someone

Someone cast a spell on me,
I wonder who could it be
oh, who could it be?

Someone makes my adrenaline pump,
and my heart race.
Every day this someone puts a smile
on my hardened face.

Someone has magically made me fall,
in love filled with the thrills…
but sometimes I wonder still
how my someone feels.

This someone has conquered all of my thoughts,
and hit me emotionally with all the right force.

My wishes were granted the day we first met
that's a day in my life I'll never forget.
She fills my days with happiness and delight,
I can't wait for the day we unite,
and hold each other tight.

She gives me a feeling I've never felt before.
Her great personality and good heart
are things that I highly adore.

There's something in her I can't even explain—
her voice, the sound of her laughter,
they make me go insane.

She's my soulmate, my lover,
my joy and my very best friend.
The connection between us
is a circle that will never end.

I hope my someone knows
how much she means to me.
I don't know what else to do
to make her see the great in me.

This someone

is one of the greatest things in my world—
I'm so happy I'm her man
and she's, my girl.

I can't find words to express
how I feel inside.

She stole my heart—
my love for her I cannot hide.

She swept me off my feet,
she's a dream come true.
Now, to be next to her
is all I want to do.

Why do I want her in a way I can't express?
Why do I think she's the best of the best?
There are so many reasons—
I could go on and on,
sunrise to sunset, dusk to dawn.

Who is this someone, you ask?
I'll tell you who…
my special someone is you.
I'm so in love with you, boo

Bound by Love

From the moment you came back into my life,
You healed a pain I could never describe.
A quiet ache that lived in the corners of my heart,
Vanished when your light shone in, bright and alive.

You are not only my best friend,
You are my wife, my partner in crime,
The laughter in my mornings,
The calm in my nights,
The reason every ordinary day feels extraordinary.

I promise to love you deeply, at God's pace
With a heart that grows with every breath,
to treat you with patience, kindness, and faith,
and to never let you feel less than cherished.

We go together like mac and cheese—
Perfect, inseparable, and complete,
two souls bound by love and laughter,
two hearts learning, growing, no longer weak

I vow never to neglect you,
Never to hurt you,
and never to walk away from you or desert you.

Through every storm, I will be your anchor,
Through every joy, I will be your echo,
holding your hand through the highs and lows,
celebrating every dream we chase together.

By God's grace, I have been given you,
And I will honor you, and protect you,
and hold you close through every trial and triumph.

You are my everything, that I need and want

My shining diamond, my eternal love,
The warmth in my winter, the calm in my drudge,
the home I always hoped to find.
I love you more than words can define
More than time can measure,
And I vow, as long as I breathe,
you will never walk alone forever

Forever Yours

I love you, baby — no ifs, ands, or maybes,
I want you forever — my wife, my lady.
It might get hazy, but I'm still crazy for you,
You're the love of my life — a dream come true.

Sometimes I don't show it, try to act all heroic,
But you're always on my mind I need you to know it.
Yeah, this long-distance life can be hard to cope with
But baby, stay focused, don't give up hope quick

I want you to stay, don't want you to leave,
I'm trying my hardest — to be the man you need.
I know what you're feeling, I feel it too,
You need your daddy there to comfort you.

We’re both waiting — just be patient, we can make it,
Look down at your bracelet when you can’t take it.
Two years ain’t nothing compared to a lifetime,
And I love putting smiles on that pretty face of mine.

Yes, I’m still attracted — matter fact, it's more,
I daydream about you and what we got in store.
That tight connection, your touch, your affection
I can’t lie, sometimes I need that private reflection.

One day soon, this wait will be done,
We’ll laugh, we’ll kiss, we’ll rise as one.
No bars, no distance, nothing between
Just me and you, living our dream.

My Love in Motion

Hey beautiful… I knew you were cool
Ever since we first met by the bar near a stool.
I said hi… then moved, I was too shy to lose
The chance to get to know you, I'm wise and smooth.

Your eyes just soothe any pain, any aches
I'm sorry for the wait, but this time it would be great.
Once I get to know you and show you…
That you're not alone in anything and everything that you'll go through.

Wanna hold you, keep you out the cold too…
Show you a love you never knew or known, boo.
The exes showed you… that a guy like me is rare
I'm not perfect, but I'm here—I show you I care.

You don't need to look no further,
don't worry
I'll earn your love and affection,
give you comfort and protection.

You don't need no other,
you made my heartbeat again
You don't have to wear mad jewelry
for me to see your gems.

You're different from the usual, your mind is right
I'm so into you, can't wait for when the time is right.
I can see you're a four-leaf clover in a field of daisies
One beautiful, focused lady, and your drive is crazy.

I'mma take my time,
making sure you get the dedicated devotion
That you deserve…
you're mine, and you know it.
Wanna walk the sands of the ocean,
holding hands
Growing into an unbreakable bond,
I wanna be your man in motion.

And when the stars shine down on us tonight
I'll hold you close, everything feels right.
Every moment with you is a gift I treasure
Forever, my love, beyond any measure.

71

The Love I Found

I thought love belonged only to others,
Each time I got close, I lost another.
I feared a broken heart—
that was the hardest part.
I faced many nights alone,
but how could I have known,
a love like ours would come around?
The end of broken hearts, I have found.
Perfect love was so hard to find,
I never knew you would be mine.
Now that I've found you,
I'll never let go.
I love every ounce of you
more than you'll ever know.

In your bed is where I want to be,
from here on, for eternity.
You are the only one I need,
you were meant to be with me.

You healed the wounds I used to hide,
you stand with me, right by my side.
The nights of pain have passed away,
your love has brought me brighter days.

I used to doubt, I used to fear,
but now I'm grateful you are here.

No more shadows, no more rain,
with you, I'm free from all the pain.
You're my shelter, my safe embrace,
my future shines when I see your face.
Together we rise, together we grow,
this kind of love I'll never outgrow.

So, take my hand, let's walk as one,
our journey has only just begun.
Through every storm, through skies so blue,
my heart belongs forever to you.

I promise to love you until my last breath,
to cherish you deeply in life and in death.
And when the world fades and all is through,
my final thought will still be *you.*

Awaiting

The days are so long
Nights are lonely
I try to be strong
My one and only
I long to feel your touch
Eyes looking into mine
Ever so sweetly
My heart begins to shine

I cradle your picture
I Read the poems
With loves mixture
I don't feel alone

So now I lie down
Smile upon my face
Awaiting the day
To feel your embrace

My soul my love
The Other part of me
Forever in my heart
you will always be

A Czar for Your Heart

You don't know what I'm trying to offer.
just Friendship and Realness, you can see
You must not be used to a guy like me.
Maybe we'll just say hi when I pass by.

It's all good. I'm not one to chase—
Though I wish I would.
want to get to know you if I could
to show I can offer more
than to fill your furnace with wood

I'm honest, earnest.
Maybe you'll see this as a lesson,
a blessing in disguise.
Be wise, cutie pie.

I'm not the type who looks for sex.
I'm deeper, want to appeal to your intellect
I want to connect—mind, heart, soul.
But all you do is text. You're cold.

No conversation. I get it.
I'm not your critic; it was nice to meet you.
Like you want, I'll find another destination.

Maybe I can teach you,
If I reach you,
See through those beautiful pupils.
I'm not your usual.

I'm not like Brutus. More like Popeye.
I love your eyes, your thighs.
I want to get high off your vibes.

You must think I'm just someone.
You use to date?
You're confused, hun.
I can take you from good to great.

I'm a man with visions.
I see myself in your life.
I have good intentions.
Maybe one day I'll give you life.

Let it grow—an oak, a maple.
I'm hopeful, praying
to show you my ways,
to see the rays I made for you,

to hear you say you'll stay
more than a day or two.

I offer a lifetime of amazement.
Devotion. Entertainment.
"Have a good day, miss."
Maybe one day, we'll kiss,

talk about brokenness,
hopelessness.
Open this gift—let it sit
on the tips of your lips.

See me as kingly, you as queen bee.
Then it'll be easier to call on me
I'll come to you wherever you are
My devotions—a book that's open.

Let me be your Czar.
I can give you more
Love, Peace, and Happiness.
Yes, you're attractive, miss, but I adore
your actions, your gifts.
I will never let you fall.

I wait for you to say yes.
To live with me. Figuratively,
I'll be okay to confess
is my answer, sincerely

I'll bless you with my caress.
I won't harm; I will heal you
May our days be filled without stress
our nights with peace to fulfill you

May love guide every step we take.
And God bless our situation.
My heart beats only for your sake
The Lord is our foundation

You Can Trust in Me

I'm not wearing all black, I won't judge you,
Because I trust in God, I will trust you
What's up with you? I know it's hard out here,
But imma help you get out of your rears,
And into the clear.

Take a chair, sit, relax, miss—
Chiropractic is my profession, I'm practicing
Yes, it's a gift from the one above
That you got, it's called love.

I can help you connect the dots,
And reach those extra spots
That they never could've got
Because they're not me.
You'll find that out eventually.
If you invest in me.

Your time and your mind
I'm designed
to find that gold sunshine.
I love to rhyme… so smile.

I know you're beautiful,
even though I don't see it.
It shows—it glows—all over the world,
Just not always at your convenience.

See, I don't need a crown or a throne,
I just need a chance to make you feel at home.
No faking, no lies, no disguise in my tone
I want you to know you're never alone.

When storms rise, I'll stand in the rain,
Praying with you, carrying your pain.
Through trials, denials, through every test,
God gave me the strength to give you, my best.

I'm not perfect, but I'm striving each day,
To love you in words and show it in unique ways.
Through trust, through faith, through fire we'll climb,
Together to eternity, beyond space and time.
So, walk with me, let's leave our fears behind,
Two souls, one purpose, our lives intertwined.
No matter the darkness, we'll always find light,
Trust in God, trust in us
And everything will be alright.

Crooked Reflections

In these last days and times,
Don't take my mind for granted.
No more love is handed; I'm stranded.
You left me… abandoned,
Without a single ounce of romance.
I never planned this way…
Now my skies are gray,
Like a bird, you chose to fly away.

Took the light from my eyes,
Left me in disgrace.
No more food on the plate,
Because you couldn't wait.
Rather call the Jakes,
trying to send me upstate
And let them claim my estates.
You laugh like this is just a game
While I'm left broken, searching
for what little dignity remains.

I stare into this crooked mirror,
Hunting for my own reflection.
Every corner of my interior
Haunted by betrayal and deception.

Yeah, it gets even weirder—than Al,
You were nasty, you were foul,
And I don’t even know if that’s my child.

I remember taking you to Mr. Chow's,
But I knew that crooked smile
would stab me in the back somehow.
Your grimy ways, your sneers, and your style

Ripped apart my heart,
Shattered my patience,
Messing up my day in trial.
I gave my trust, my care, and you flaked it.
You spat on it, stomped on it,
Left me crawling in the ashes
Of what we used to call love.
Now bitterness and harassment

Like a storm that won’t end,
And the pain—oh, the pain
It is a constant, bitter friend.
I'm stuck in the rain.
Every laugh you faked,
Every lie that you whispered,

Burns in my mind
Like bleach on raw flesh.

All by your design
You took what wasn't yours to take,
Left me empty,
Left me to ache,
Left me with nothing but fury.

No way to escape
I hope the weight of your choices
Crushes you someday,
Like you crushed me.
I hope the crooked smiles you wear
Turn into sneers that haunt me.

I hope you feel the sting.
Of every deceitful move you made.
And yet… I rise,
Even in this hatred and rage,
I carve my reflection from the mirror,

Piece by broken piece,
And swear I will never hand my heart
to a cruel, obese beast
Crooked reflections fade eventually,
But the lessons remain sharp,
And I will survive.
Like it was meant for me

Hi/bye

I just wanted to greet you,
but I'll kindly delete you.
It was nice to meet you,

I know not to call you
to ask you to help me.
If I were homeless, wouldn't shelter me
If I were on fire,
You wouldn’t pee on me
to put out the flames easily.

You would rather watch me burn or hang.
I don't know what I did to you,
But you assume the wrong thing.

It's okay, the signs I see
I will go away and leave in vain
like the pain, when Aleve hits my veins.

I understand you hate me as a man,
and you think I have mischievous plans.
I know I'm sincere and pure and grand.
But you don't seem to understand

So have a nice life.
I won't bother you
with my problems, too.
I know your world revolves around you.
I'm through.

Mackerel

To be my mackerel
I need half of your soul.
I'll give you whatever you ask, for your goals,
But you better have my dough and be accurate, Yō.
It's a pledge to me to have my back for growth.
You gotta be above average though,
You gotta match my flow,
And have my gold.
As I've been told, from what I teach you,
I have many goals; we could never be equal.
Because the highest quality that I see in you,
Why equals equality? I foresee it in you.
I believe it's true
And I see it in you.

You're beautiful,
But I will have you buying me all I need too.

My perfection offers no apologies.
I'm astonished and intrigued
by your bionic ideologies and degrees.
If I were to offer you my analogies,
would you still have followed me?

Would you still keep pace with my rhythm,
or let the music fade before the harmony begins?
I want your mind, your focus, your vision,
as much as your heart and your ambition.

Not just your surface, not just your charm,
I want that fire that keeps you warm.
I want to see you rise, to see you shine,
to build a world where your light aligns with mine.

I need loyalty, honesty, the raw, the real,
a connection that only we could feel.
I need you to challenge me,
to push me past what I thought I could be,
to see the spark that fuels my soul,
to grow together, making each other whole.

Half of your soul, half of mine,
blended in passion, in purpose, in time.
Late-night pillow talks, the plans we design,
the laughter, the love, we perfectly align.

The journey isn’t simple, the ocean isn’t calm,
but together, we will weather storms, hands in palms.
Every step, every risk, every vow we take,
I’ll hold you close, every move we make.

So, tell me, my mackerel,
will you step into this ocean with me?
I need more than half of your soul
together, we're unstoppable, in peace.

Thanks

Thanks for coming by, Miss Fly,
I appreciated it
the greatest gift
of dedication and devotion
a moment
That eased my hopelessness.
Even if it was just for one minute,
I was fulfilled, thrilled, replenished
by your genuine grin,
‘cause you wanna see me win, win, win,
like DJ Khaled, no matter what predicament I’m in
Or how this case may end.
I’m an M&M-flavored emblem,
embracing your presence
like a fresh essence,
seeds to a salad.
Without you, I'll be breathless
Good looking, good looking.
Enjoy your New Year’s.
Overcome your new fears
with conviction,
purpose, and vision
’Cause you can’t trust all your friends

to keep your deepest secrets
when you're on the deep end.
They'll turn shallow, hollow,
let the creaks creep in
like weak links.
But you're strong like Cuban links.
You'll never let them break away the chains,
or take away the pain,
Or fade away like Chef treys.
But you're strong like Cuban links.
You'll never let them break away the chains,
or take away the pain,
Or fade away like Chef treys.
Thanks for letting me hold onto my faith.
I can put my trust in you
When I'm in pain on those rainy days,
When the floods come through
when I just wanna throw it all away,
Thanks.
I know you're gonna do what you need to do
to make sure I don't lose
'cause you need a pursc too.
Being honest is virtual,
onyx is your birthstone.
With purity, personally, I'll reimburse you

I'm thankful for your service,
for serving me with quality.
You deserve a raise in salary
for helping me reliably

Every day you fought
for my rights like Rocky,
with diligence and conviction
like you were locked up illegally in Philly FDC.

For helping me
They treat you like a villainess
I respect your hustler mentality.
You're not just any lawyer,
You're an employer with a God morality
I love your integrity.
You deserve that one-third fee —
Your record proceeds
You're way better than me
People don't see
all the hard work you put in;
can't see the proof in the pudding,
they only want results,
not the truth you are pursuing.

Forever, For Now

Sunlight creepin' through the blinds
like it was shy,
your leg draped over mine,
breathing slow, no lie.

Lie down.
No liquor talk, no sneaky link,
just me and you to the brink.
Your stresses are released from this BBC.
Your curls on my chest, relieved.
your laughs in my ear,
no regrets, no games,
just the truth that we both wanted to hear.
simple and plain
I'm not just chasing bodies.
I’m chasing your mind,
your rhythm, your behind, your past,
all intertwined.

You ask if I’m serious.
and I kiss your doubts away,
saying I’m not just here for the night...
Baby, I’m here to stay.

We talk about our dreams,
We talk about our pain.
We talk about kids and their names.
and how our life can be rearranged.

We talk about how love isn’t perfect.
But this?
This is what it is.
This is worth it.

I make breakfast while you daydream.
You're wearing my tee.
I swear, the way I made you scream
I knew you wouldn't want to leave.
I never knew a peace of mind.
could look like you're behind.
You tell me your secrets; I tell you mine.
We laughed at the mess we made.
while we sipped on some wine.

Talked about our plans for the rest of the day;
...I lied about mine.
I save your name in my phone with a heart.
You say, "Don’t play with me.”
but I already did,

I was playing my part.

You say you've never felt this safe, this seen,
and I say, "Me neither."
though I've routinely said that routine.

We walk through the park; fingers locked like fate.
You say, "Promise me this isn't just first-date bait."
I say, "I promise."
and I mean it... for now.
But promises bend.
when the past comes back around.

Later that night, I'm alone in my car,
your scent on my hoodie,
your voice in my palm.
I scroll through my texts.
to see what's next.

I see three unread messages.
three girls I ghosted, acting like pests

I stared at your photo, the one you just sent.
captioned "forever,"
but I know what that meant.

I'm a lover, a liar, a poet, and a thief.
I give you, my truth.
Then I steal your belief.

I wanted to change.
I swear that I tried.
but love's just a story
I reply, then deny.

So, I drive to her crib,
the one from last June,
the one who still calls me
her sun and her moon.
If I knocked on her door
and said, "I'm back for good."
Her face would light up.
like I knew that it should.

But before I knocked on her door,
I deleted your name from my phone.
Put her name as wifey,
and sprayed my jock with cologne.
But you changed my mind.
and I drove away like a ghost.

in the city's glow,
just before my hooptie got towed.

The texts I sent were a silent promise.
I'll break another day.
My next destination
is the one where no one knows my face,
where I can't be found
by the people who knows my game.

I even lie to myself.
thinking I can be confined to a wife.
I tried to get help.
but it only lasts for a night.

I'm a master of beginnings,
an artist of the first act,
and the curtain is always about to fall back,
My emotions are never intact.

The past isn't something I run from;
It's a home I can't ever return to.
and the future is just another stranger.
waiting to burn you.

100

My only true love
is the moment before the fall,
the quiet before the storm,
the sweet illusion of forevermore.

Because in the end,
I'm only ever truly with myself—
my enemy and my friend,
a lonely book on the shelf
that never seems to end.

Flawless

You're flawless and gorgeous,
Sexy, smooth, and feisty like a Porsche is.
Being away from you is so torturous,
You're awesome,
I just had to break in your fortress.

I'll steal your heart,
I knew you were real from the start.
I dread the day that we should ever part.

You're the first one
to make me feel whole and complete.
What we have is so deep,
you would never have to compete.
I am not perfect, I have my weaknesses and flaws,
But I'm real, hard as steel, and all yours.
You're my queen in my eyes, heart, and mind.
I guarantee you that we will be just fine.

If you play your part and make me happy,
I will forever hold your heart and be your daddy.
But every relationship takes work to work,
You've got to be patient, miss, I learned it works.

I love that you're love-oriented
and strawberry scented.
The fact that you want a better life,

I hope you're ready for this.
You give me that satisfaction,
my conscience was accurate.
Every time I kiss you,
my heart does backflips.

It seems too good to be true,
I'm living out my dreams
with the woman of my dreams;
she's a drug, I'm a fiend.
I can't stop thinking of you,
I love to love you.
Yes, it's all about you,
I put no one else above you.

Whether it's just chilling at the crib
watching your eyes,
I'm going to be there, alright?
I don't ever wanna see you cry.
I wanna live up in your ribs
'til the sunrise, I don't mind.

103

With you, time stands still,
hours evaporate.
I have so much faith
even though we moved at a faster pace.
We're both hopeless romantics,
we couldn't have planned this.
The way our love shines like diamonds
that will never vanish.
I know I don't have all the right answers.
And I'm an emotional cancer
that tries to be outlandish,
yet you somehow find a way to understand it.
There isn't another woman on this entire planet
That I would want to be with;
you gave me enough chances.

I only wanna make you happy,
tell me what I need to do.
To be with you,
I'll crawl to the bottom of the sea with cement shoes.
I have to see a mental health professional,
because you drive me crazy; I have mean issues.
But at least you don't judge me
or hold a grudge with me.
You always stayed by my side when things got ugly.

104

You're flawless;
I don't even know what to call this,
this feeling that I have for you.
I'm a Love-a-holic.

If you could pause this, I would stay
Right here every day,
don't care what no one says.
I'm socially insane
because I'm hoping in a way
That everyone else dies except you and I,
sort of like a suicide.

I've got you inside my mind, body, and soul.
If truth be told, I'd probably be a toad
Just to be your prince, you've got me convinced

That you're my queen that was heaven sent
from the essence, miss.
You're a diamond without blemishes,
that's evident — pure excellence.

Venus In My Vision

You came through my life like lightning...
fierce and furious,
A crook of my heart,
now you've got me curious.

I saw you on the screen, but I felt you in my chest,
Your voice hit my soul — I knew I would never rest.

I ain't got time for games or lies, I'm here to build,
A future with fire, with passion fulfilled.

Let's cut off the past, and let the exes fade,
We're flexin' now, in the love that we made.

Tell me you're loyal, tell me you will stay,
When the world turns cold, don't ever drift away.
I'll give you my time, my truth, and my flames,
No matter the reason or the season,
I'll call on your name.

Miss Venus, let's play — not tennis, but fate,
You're the key to my locks, the food on my plate.

I ain't aged in a minute, I'm still young in my heart,
With you on my team, we're a work of art.

Overdue Love

It's been over seven years
since my last real love begun,
and truth be told, it hasn't all been fun.
I told myself I was waiting for the right one,
but dating drained me...
felt like fluid in my right lung.

The scene was toxic, cold, and mean,
These women were wild where I come from
no in-between.
Still, I held my head high, kept my self-esteem,
never asleep, but chasing those elusive dreams

Then I met this girl her, name was Hazel,
Eyes hypnotic, her vibe? Untamable.
She was overqualified, too rare to pass by,
Couldn't let another lonely day go bye.

I survived the toughest blocks,
and the concrete jungles of Amerikkka,
But her rejections from her?
Man, she had me in terror bruh.

Was it miscommunication or something deeper?
I was losing sleep, emotions running steeper.

I was high on hope, low from the waiting,
Patiently hating, quietly breaking,
wishing she'd end that fugazi situation
So I could be her real foundation.

Maybe it was just my imagination,
But I kept building up this anticipation.
I dreamed of the day
when this would all make sense —
No more distance, no more defenses.

It's been a while since I truly smiled,
That spark first lit when I saw her profile.
But I won't fold, and I won't throw in the towel,
No one else compares... I don't want another now.

I'd sacrifice my peace, even risk my pride,
to make her dreams cum true with me by her side.
I don't need anyone else — no substitute will do,
Because Hazel, I only one I want is **you!**

Happy Belated V-Day, Miss

Happy belated V-Day, baby
It's better late than never,
No, I'm not crazy...
Well, maybe
I've just been waiting for you... like, forever.

I just knew you were meant to be mine
Right now, not later, not down the line.
I waited patiently all this time
Just to ask if you'd be my Valentine.
Would you intertwine with my lifestyle?
Let me inside your mind, let's ride it out
It wouldn't be a crime — you see the signs.
And I know you feel it too… you ain't blind.
The view looks better with you in the frame,
Don't be shy — don't play any games.
Let me spend forever with you,
And whatever on you.
Not just because I'm light-skinned
Tall, handsome, with a nice grin,
but because I'm loyal to a fault,
paid your ransoms, handle your thoughts.
Of course I'm late...
We hadn't met on that date.
But this is a creation of elation —
Heaven-sent, no debate.

OMG — I know you smell me,
Like I'm heaven's scent,
fresh with Frankincense.
Ever since I saw your pic,
I could picture you with me — ever since.

I'm not here to confuse you,
But I promise, I'm nothing like what you're used to.
I got more drive than a Subaru,
I'm not of this new school
I'm a dinosaur —Kinda sure
You're chased by dudes who use, then ignore.
But not no more.
I'm not here to down you —
I'm here to crown you.
Not devalue you —
But devour and empower you.
I want to romance you
like a Cancer do,
hold hands with you,
Because the answer is YOU.

111

You’re the riddle to my mystery,
The peace to my misery.
I prayed every night —
"Lord, please send me a wife."
The you appeared like you was sent to me

I want to be the yin to your yang,
The pen to your ink
So I wrote this poem
to give you something to think...

About life.
About this throne.
About this vision
Where you’re not alone.
And my name gets mentioned

Picture me beside you — in symmetry.
Ideally, that’s how it’s meant to be.
Don’t fight the light that’s shown —
Just let it be known.
Happy belated Valentine’s Day.
If you were mine, you’d never wait.
Not just sweets on February 14th —
But **every single day**.

Cheers... to wow and smiles,
Because that's my style.
I'll love you out loud,
Live out those vows

I'd alleviate your stress and pain,
Never deviate, or play mind games.
I'm real and thrilled
To fill that space you've concealed.

I'm digging your vibes, I'm ready to collide —
Heart to heart, mind to mind.
You will feel divine,
Like you've been blessed
by the Most High.
No disrespect,
But I'm coming for your neck, bow ties.
I vow to make you smile,
And be proud of your future king.
I'll lift you out of the usual thing
If you'll just let me call you Queen.
Happy belated Valentine's, miss.
My love and affection?
Timeless and **progressive**.
No Wi-Fi needed —

This connection can't be intercepted.
Once you accept it,
Expect to be with the best, miss.
Let me be the answer to your lessons,
The romancer to your blessings,
An enhancement to your successes.
You'll never be abandoned,
Nor neglected.

Happy Valentine's, miss.
May our chemistry be everlasting.
And may you never forget this
This passionate gift…

If heaven ever asked it.

You Came Back

I can’t explain the pain you healed
The day you came back, love was revealed.
You stir my soul, you make me whole,
My dearest friend, my heart, my goal.

Through lonely nights I dreamed of you,
Of all the things that we would do.
One thing is for certain, pure and bright:
I’ll always love you and hold you tight.

Like beans and rice, we are meant to be,
Two souls entwined in harmony.
In every hug, I find my home,
With you, I’ll never feel alone.

You are the gift I don’t deserve,
By God’s own grace, I’ve found this nerve.
My shining diamond, rare and true,
Forever, love, I will cherish you.

It's Your Birthday

To the One I Love the Most

It's your birthday...
But I'm the lucky one,
To have spent another year
by your side.

It's your birthday...
and with each passing year,
You become more wonderful,
you are the prize.

It's your birthday...
And I'm so thankful
For these past three years
We've shared together.

It's your birthday...
And every single day,
I find my love for you
Growing deeper and better.

It's your birthday...
And I look ahead with joy
To every moment,
every memory we've yet to do.

It's your birthday...
And I wonder how I ever lived
Through all those years
Without knowing you.

It's your birthday...
And no matter what fate holds,
I know I'll be okay
as long as I have you.

It's your birthday...—
But I got the gift:
You — in my life,
For another year with my boo.

Here's to many more birthdays together,
Many more reasons to celebrate you.

Happy Birthday, baby,

Side Eyes & Solid Ground

Sorry for the things I said...
But I felt them.
I messed up
I fell in love with you,
And I couldn't help it.
I wanted you all to myself...
I was selfish.
Even though I stood tall
without you I felt elfish

I believed everything you said
About us,
About family,
About forever.
You were all in my head.

Or maybe that's just the Cancer in me
or my insanity.
You told me you'd never leave me Randomly.
Maybe you were misunderstanding me,
But I can admit, I underhandedly
believed in a romantic fantasy.
Oh so simple, can't it be!

I don’t think so.
Not in these days and times
Where vanity rules the soul.
Where people in cruise control
Ghost you, like removing a post

But it’s all God.
I’m not mad at you.
It’s your loss
Her gain.
Pain raised me,
Taught me how to stand in the rain.
Still, I thank God
For blessing me handsomely.
I will recover.
I overstand and see,
And on solid God rock
I will land on my feet
You said you needed space,
So I’ll give you a whole galaxy.
I love you,
but I gotta go, I gotta leave.
I can’t accept being a French fry side guy.
So…
Have a nice life. 👍
Side eyes. 👀

My Shining Diamond

I could never explain the pain that helped my happiness decay. The one that settled in my bones and turned every day to gray. It was a silence that lived deep within me, an empty space where your laughter used to be. But the day you came back, that silence shattered. It was more than a moment; it was a revelation that mattered. Love wasn't just a feeling; it was a force that rushed in and filled every broken part of me that was corrupted. You didn't just return; you breathed new life into my universe. You ruined my hurt with a single glance, and in your presence, you make me feel like a champ. My dearest friend, my true heart, my ultimate goal. I went from hopeless to hopeful, to the top of your totem pole.

In all those lonely nights, you were my only dream. The only one I wanted to wake up to, that would make me serene. I was lost in visions of our future with you forever, of all the simple, beautiful things that we would do together. Now, with you beside me, I know things are pure, and bright: I will always love you, always hold you tight. We fit together like the moon and the night—a perfect, humble harmony, a union that just makes all right.

In every kiss, I find my bliss, a sanctuary from the world problems, and with you in my arms, I know I'll never feel alone again. I promise.

You are the precious gift that I don't deserve. a miracle found through a grace, which i can't put into words. I can't explain. By some divine hand, I've been given the nerve to reach for you and hold you close and speak to you. You are my shining diamond, rare and true, a light that guides my way through and reflects in the hue. All the love that I have I will give to you Forever, my love, I will cherish you.

Sucker4Love 4ever

Thanks, God, for she I was a lost fish at sea.
She came like a mermaid, helped me see.
I was swimming in deep waters of self-torture,
just another fish, schooled by the wrought of love,
drowning in a pool of awful thoughts
lost in the sauce.
I thought that love was a game,
I fought, and I lost

But she saved me from sharks and eels that prey
I was electrified by the Morays,
until they sting me in my face

I was prone to trouble,
lonely and vulnerable.
but unlike a clone, she was lovable,
but I was gullible

she was real, my shield
my armor, who armed me with devotion.
she was a drug that was potent,
that was smoothed as lotion.
Soft spoken, she derailed my hopelessness,
helped me refocus
on the dreams, at least notice them.

Let me not forget to mention
she was beautiful, flawless with no blemishes.
More than a friend with benefits
she finished my sentences

that had been left broken
since the rages of youth, misused power.
I sprung open like a flower
when she devoured the cowards

that used to prey on me;
she empowered me in prayer.
she was well seasoned I just added some flavor

Then one day she walked
back to the shore and mimed,
"It wasn't you; it was me."
She wasn't sure she could be mine.

She was tangled in her own storms,
not ready to commit to this;
and if it's His will, maybe it'll be revisited.
but I didn't have patience, just sickness

So, I tripped, fell into some bull ish
flipped and sent texts
vexed with vindictiveness., she wasn't so innocent.
Apologies came, but they were not accepted.
It was my fault; I overthought her messages.

Not I'm back to being lonely with no one to hold me
I cut off all me thots to make her my one and only
maybe I'm just prone to be
a sucker4love too
because I keep letting emotions take control of me…

F🖕c$ You!!!

About Author:

Coolgmack is more than a poet—he's a voice carved out of the concrete jungles of Westchester and NYC, the so-called "melting pot of ruin." Raised through group homes, jails, and institutions, he learned early that the streets can teach you just as much as any classroom—only harsher. After graduating from Sleepy Hollow High in '97, the pull of New York's darker corners dragged him into Rikers Island, robbing him of his prime but igniting the fire that would shape his destiny.

Years spent inside cages could have broken him—but instead, he chose to sharpen his words into weapons of truth. Poetry became his sanctuary, his megaphone, his redemption. While serving an unjust, perpetual sentence (smh), Coolgmack vowed to flip his pain into purpose. His verses carry the grit of survival, the ache of injustice, and the hope of transformation.

Today, he writes not just to heal himself but to uplift communities caught in the same cycle. His mission is unity, strength, and the reminder that your circumstances don't define your future. A poet, author, publisher, and entrepreneur, Coolgmack is on a mission to spark revolution through revelation—helping others uncover their inner talents and believe in more than the struggle.

You can find him everywhere the ink spills—Instagram, Facebook, Amazon, or at **coolgmack.com**. Step inside his books , including his latest drop *Sucker4Love Too*, and witness the holy fusion of pain, passion, and purpose.

the author Coolgmack has written the following books:

- **Sucker4pain vol. 1: Tales of Love That Hurt Too Good:** This is described as a "gritty, uncut testimony" from a man who has experienced betrayal and heartbreak. It's a collection of poetry exploring themes of love, addiction, prison, and faith.
- **Sucker4lust vol.1: The Sweet Scent of sin and salvation:** This book, described as a book that explores themes of sin, salvation, and the scent of sweet lust.
- **Psalms in my Palm:** A devotional companion for those in pain a collection of prayers and poetic reflections by Coolgmack. The book, born from the author's personal journey through hardship, blends lyrical devotion with scripture, offering a guide toward God's light. It's for anyone who feels broken and is longing to be reminded that they are seen and never alone.
- **Poetic Injustices in Amerikkka:** This book is a work of "poetic American Analysis" that addresses racial inequality and institutional racism. It aims to provide a firsthand insight into these issues and calls for social and economic change for Black Americans.
- **Sucker4drugs: Confessions, Consequences, and Recovery:** This book is a collection of poetry that chronicles a journey through addiction, despair, and the pursuit of recovery. It covers themes of substance abuse, incarceration, and ultimately, hope and redemption.
- **Chronicles of a Hangry Black Soul:** This is a collection of poetry that documents a life "in a perpetual state of hunger—not for food, but for truth, justice, and spiritual liberation." It includes themes of social and spiritual commentary, the prison system, relationships, and personal healing.
- **Sucker4love:** This book is a collection of original poems that narrate the author's journey through love and heartbreak, also sharing memories of true love and hope.

www.ingramcontent.com/pod-product-compliance
Lightning Source LLC
Chambersburg PA
CBHW071532100726
47908CB00004B/1373

* 9 7 9 8 9 9 3 0 0 4 6 2 4 *